According to recent research, coloring a drawing helps reduce anxiety. We have many reasons to be anxious, to some extent it is a normal reaction of our body, but there are cases in which anxiety begins to interfere with everyday activities. This book is a valuable tip to calm your thoughts and feel a little satisfaction. Have fun coloring these beautiful flowers.

Franciele Caires

2024

This Book Belongs to:

○————————————————————————————————○

Test Color Page

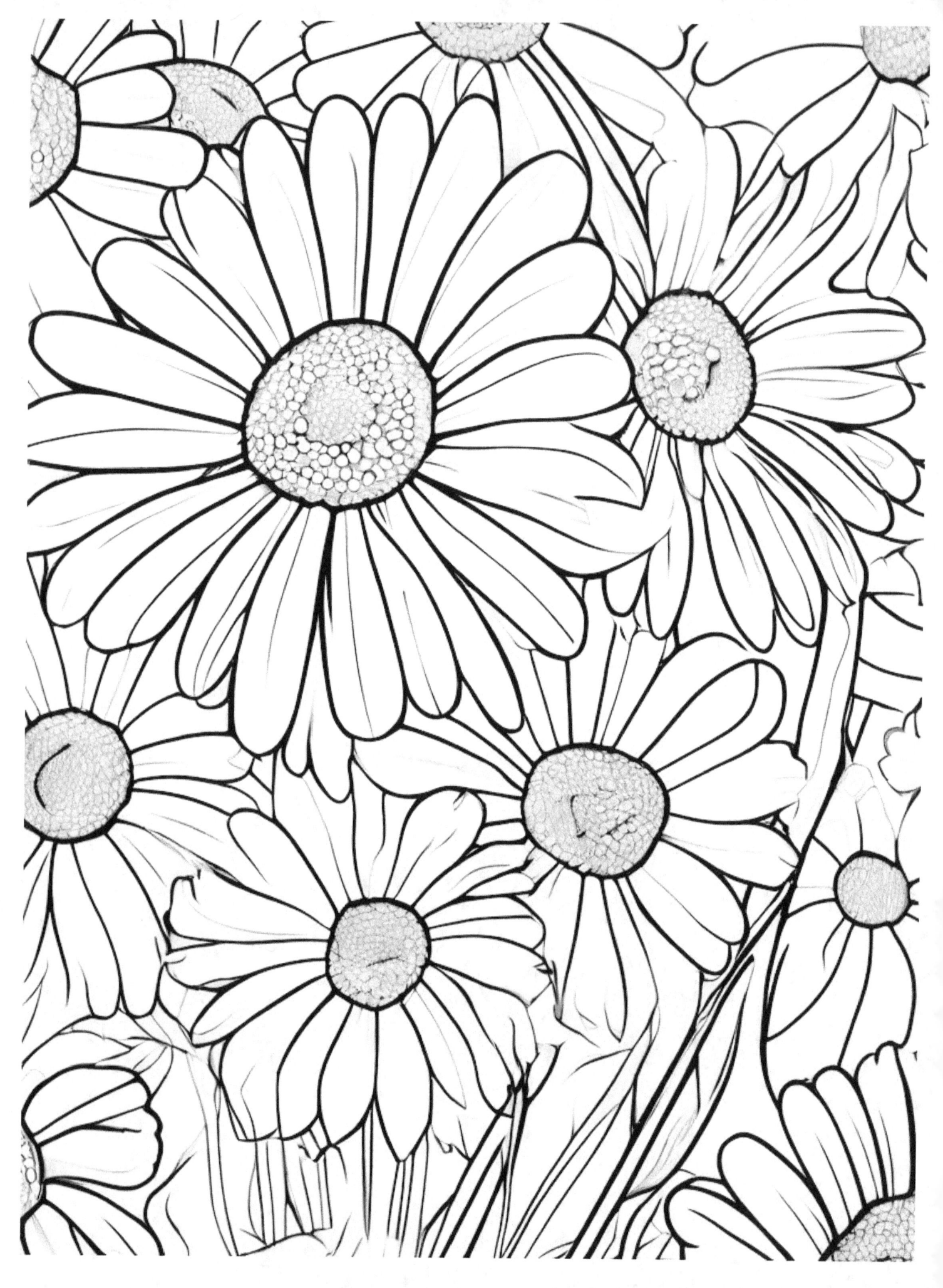

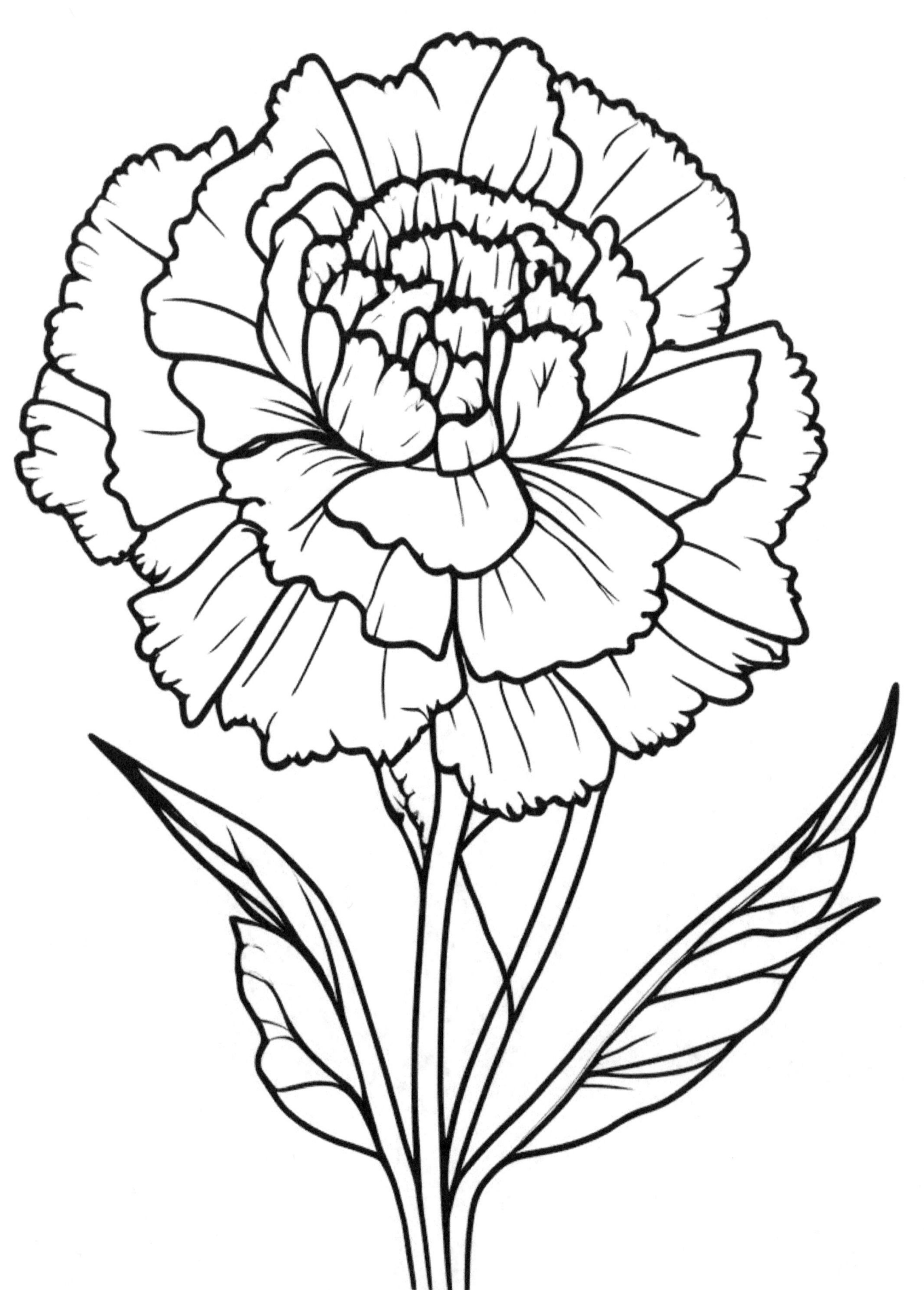

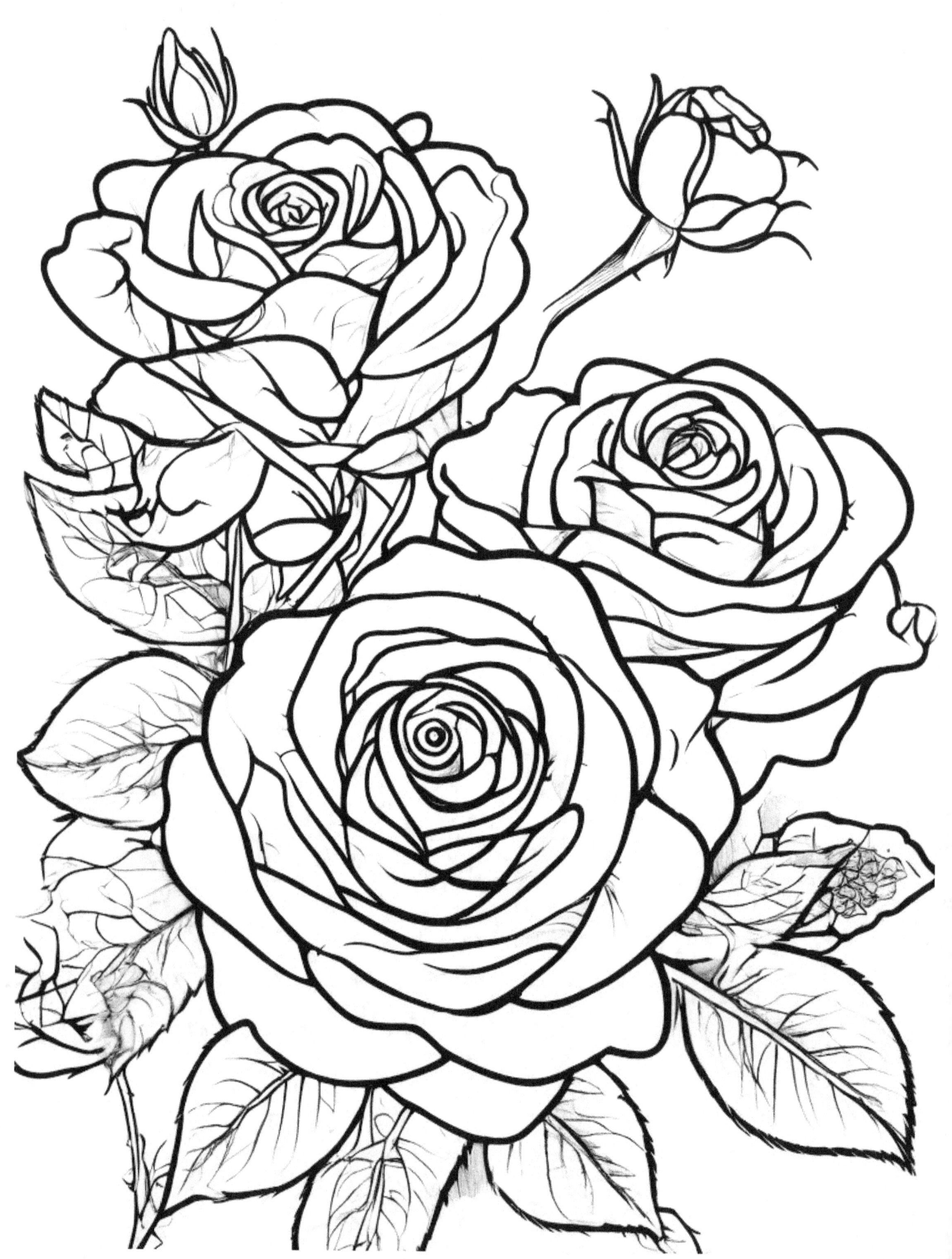

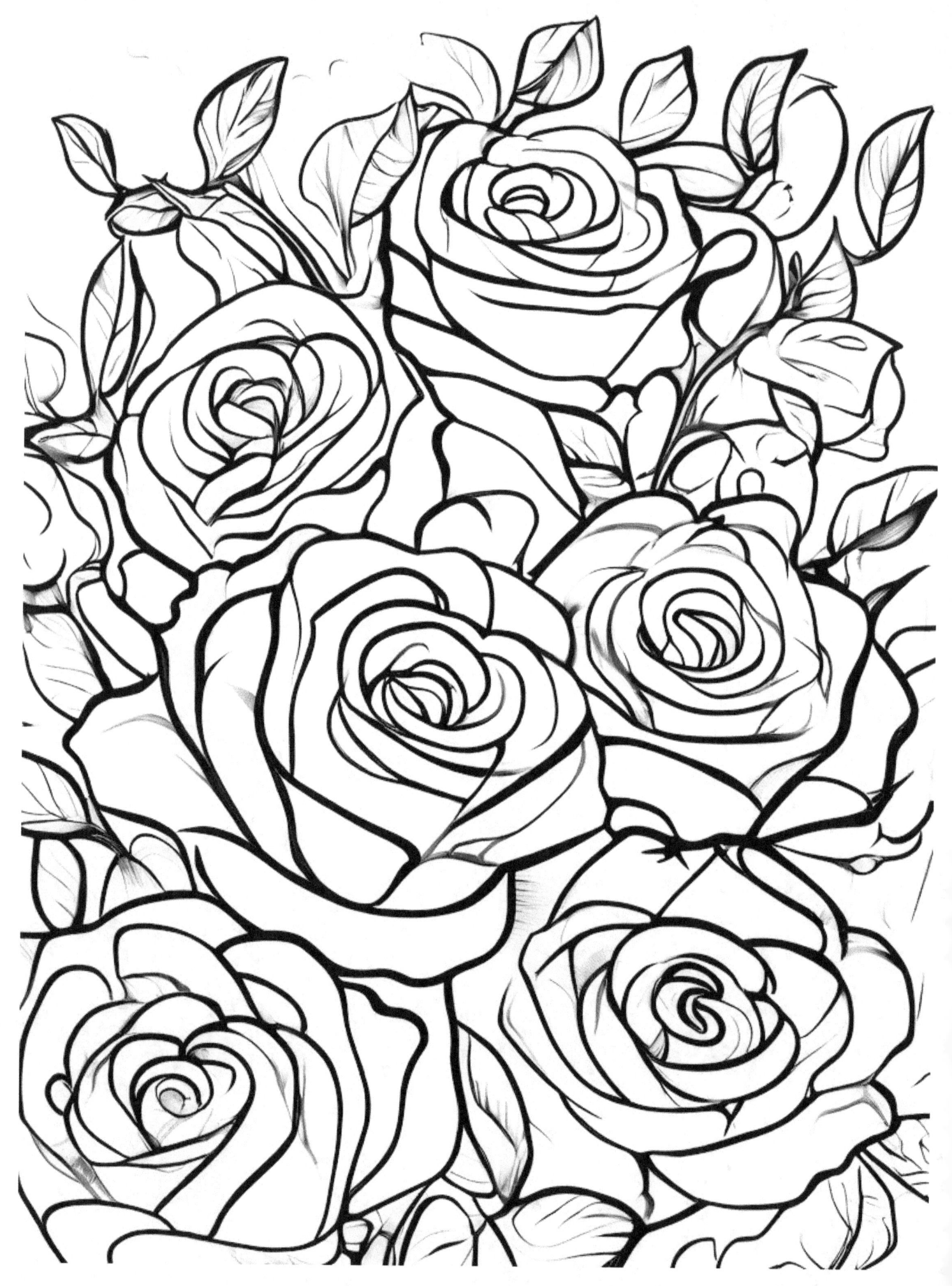

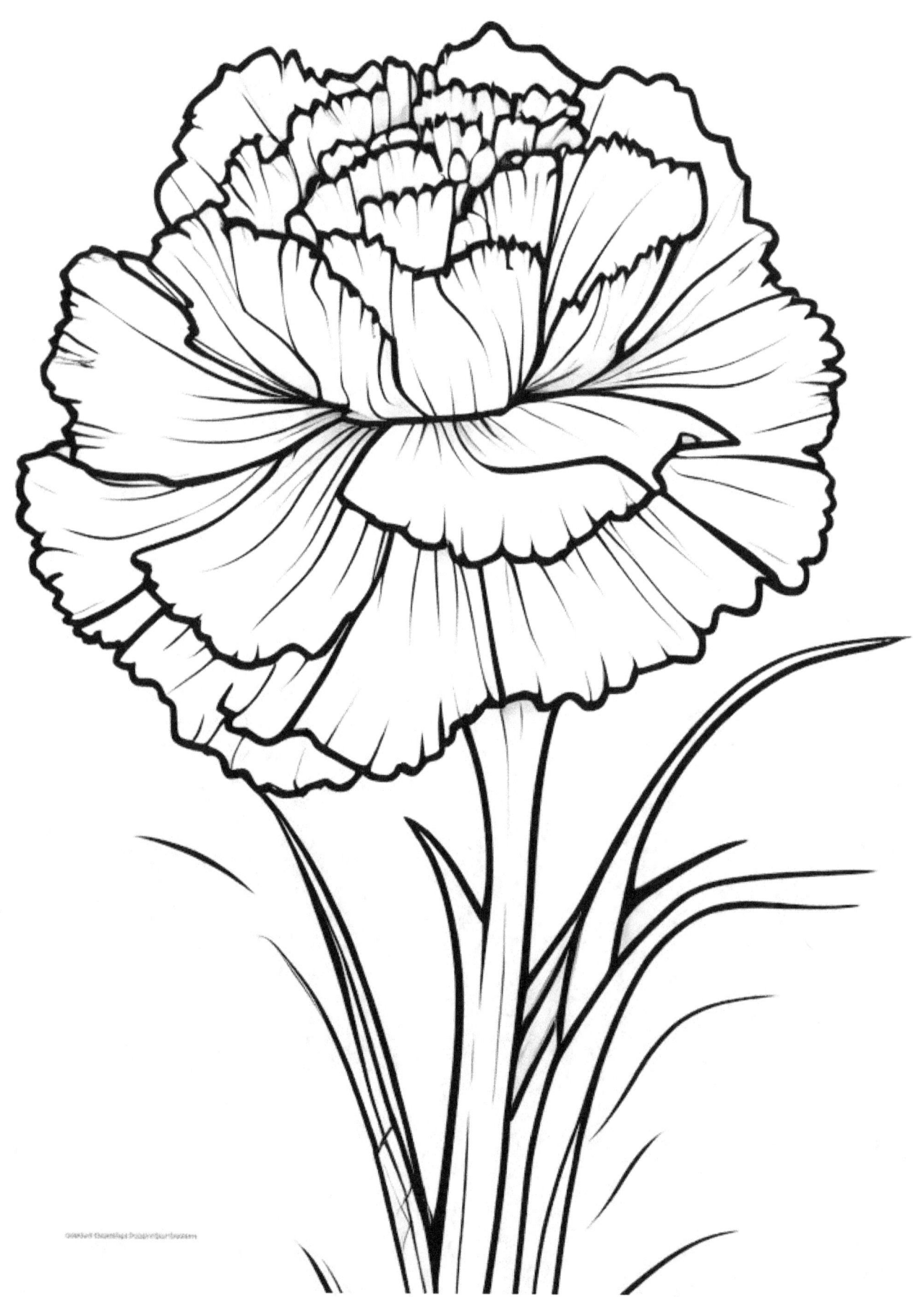

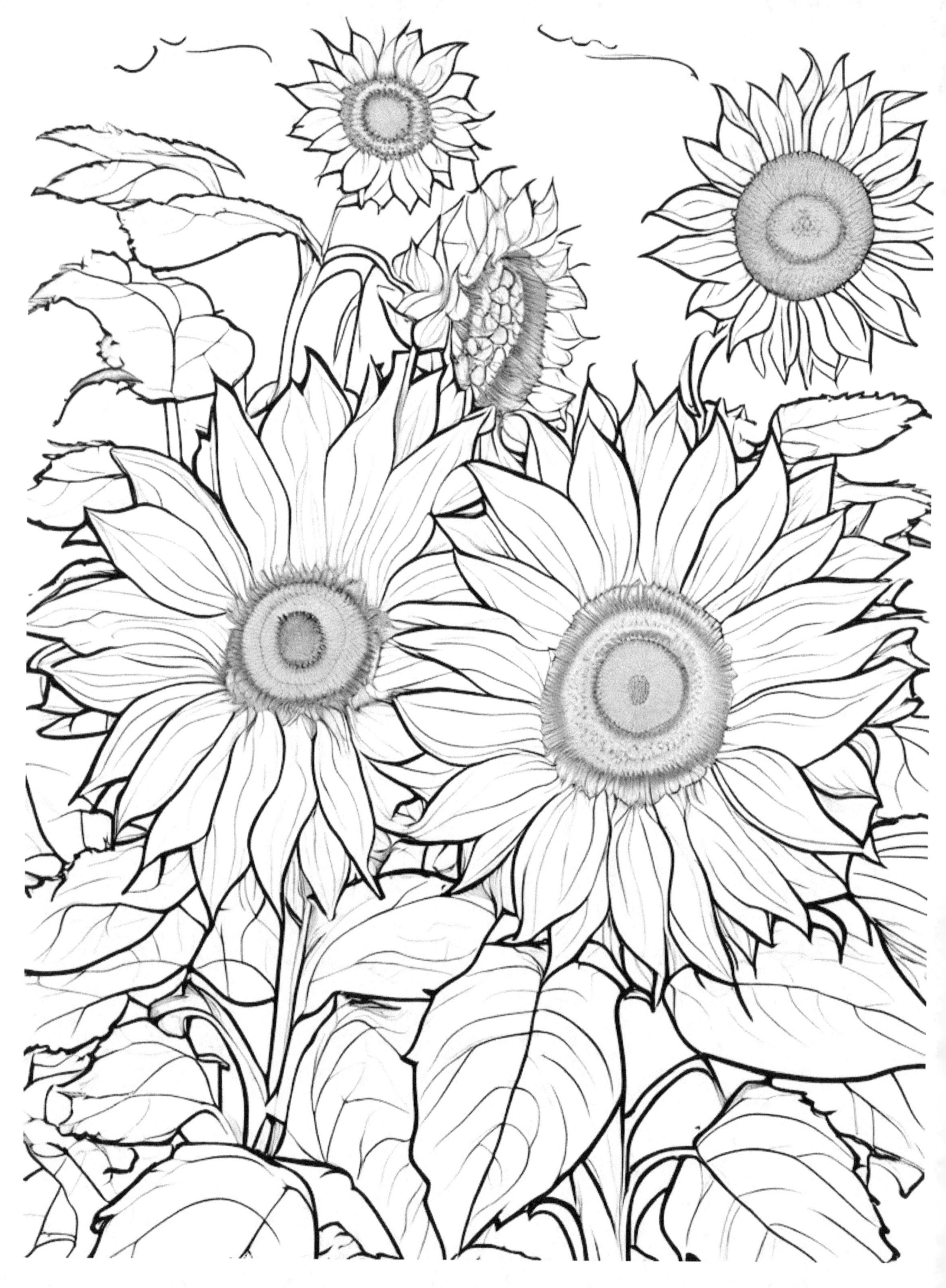

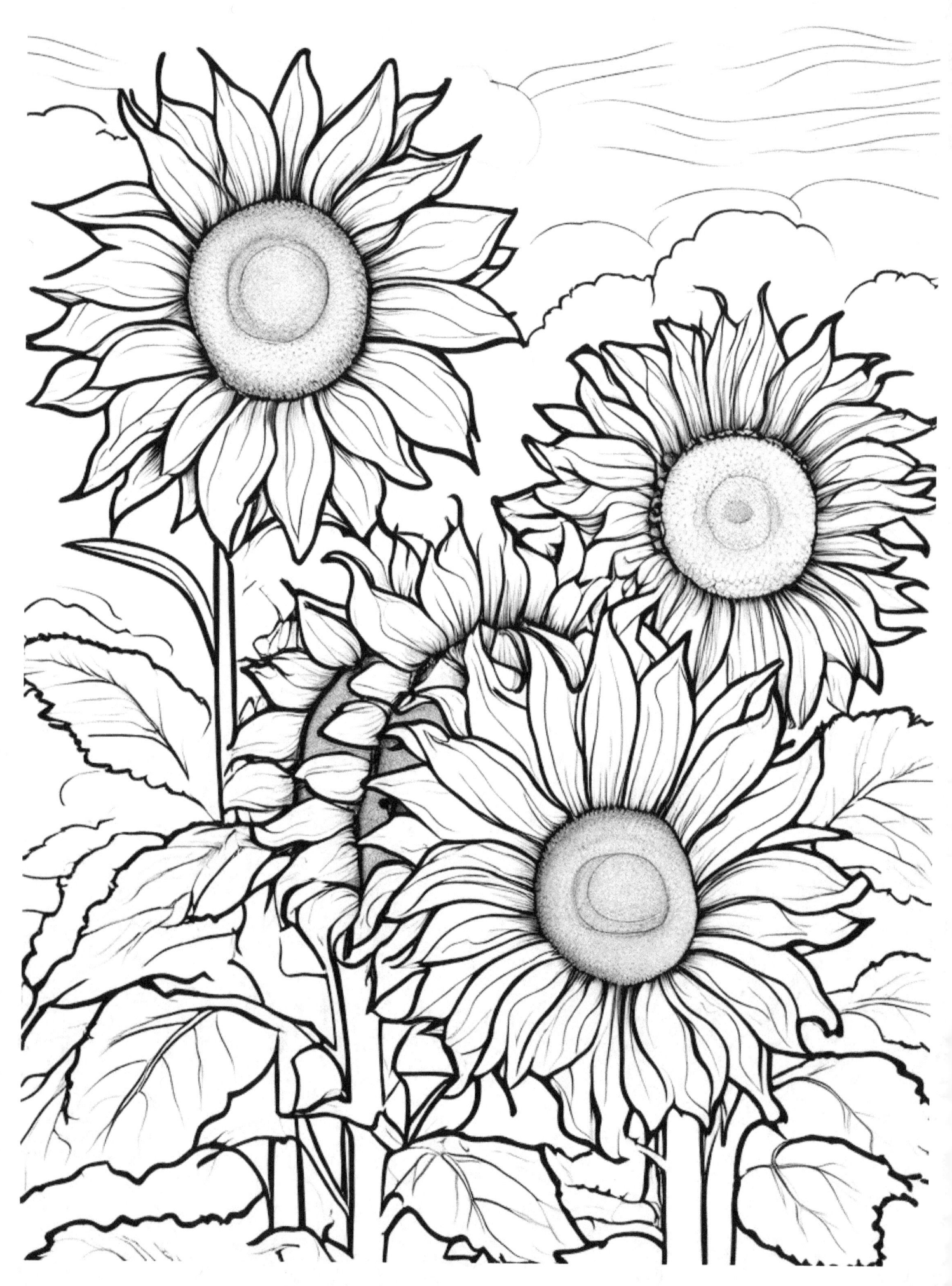

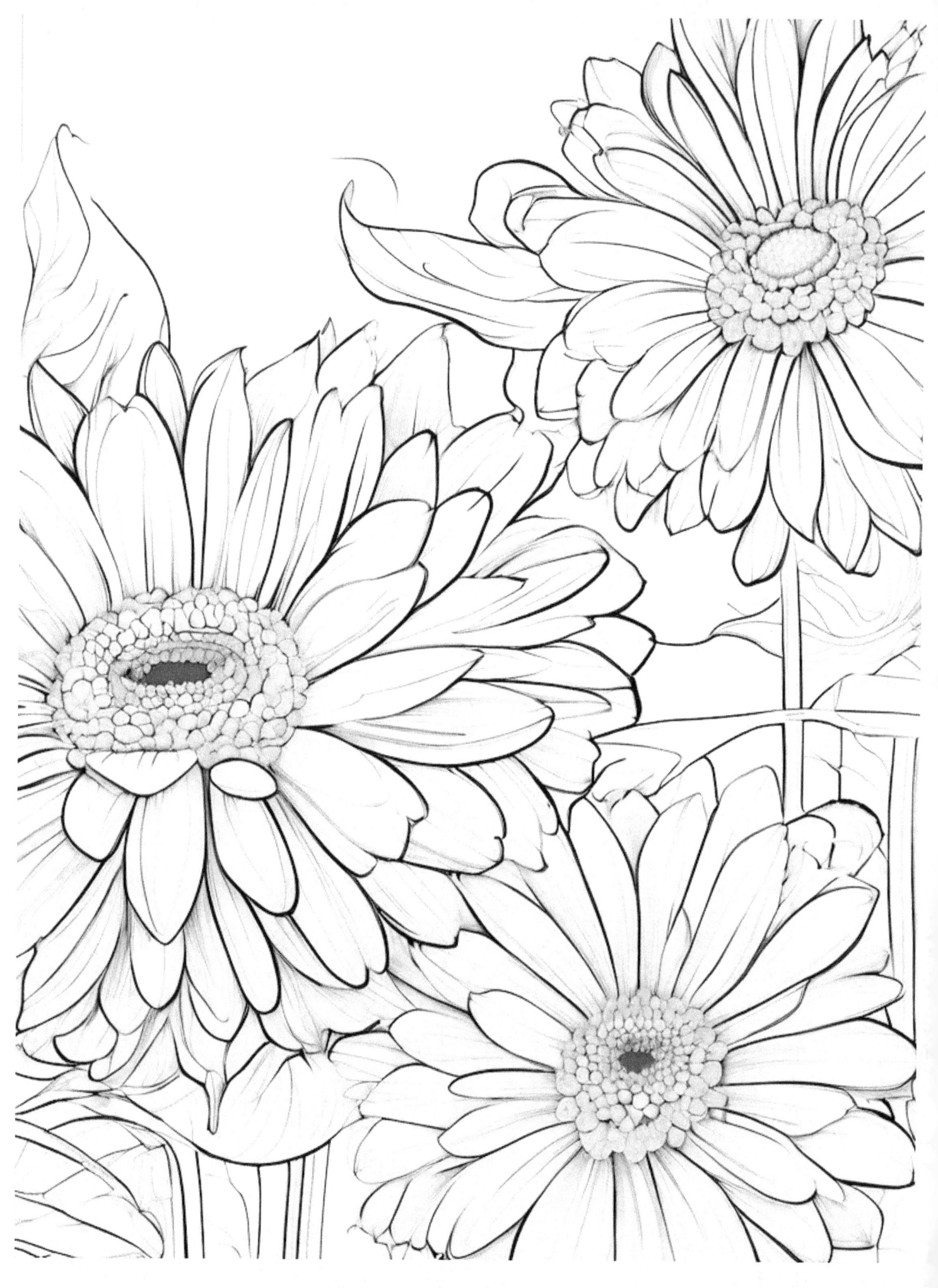

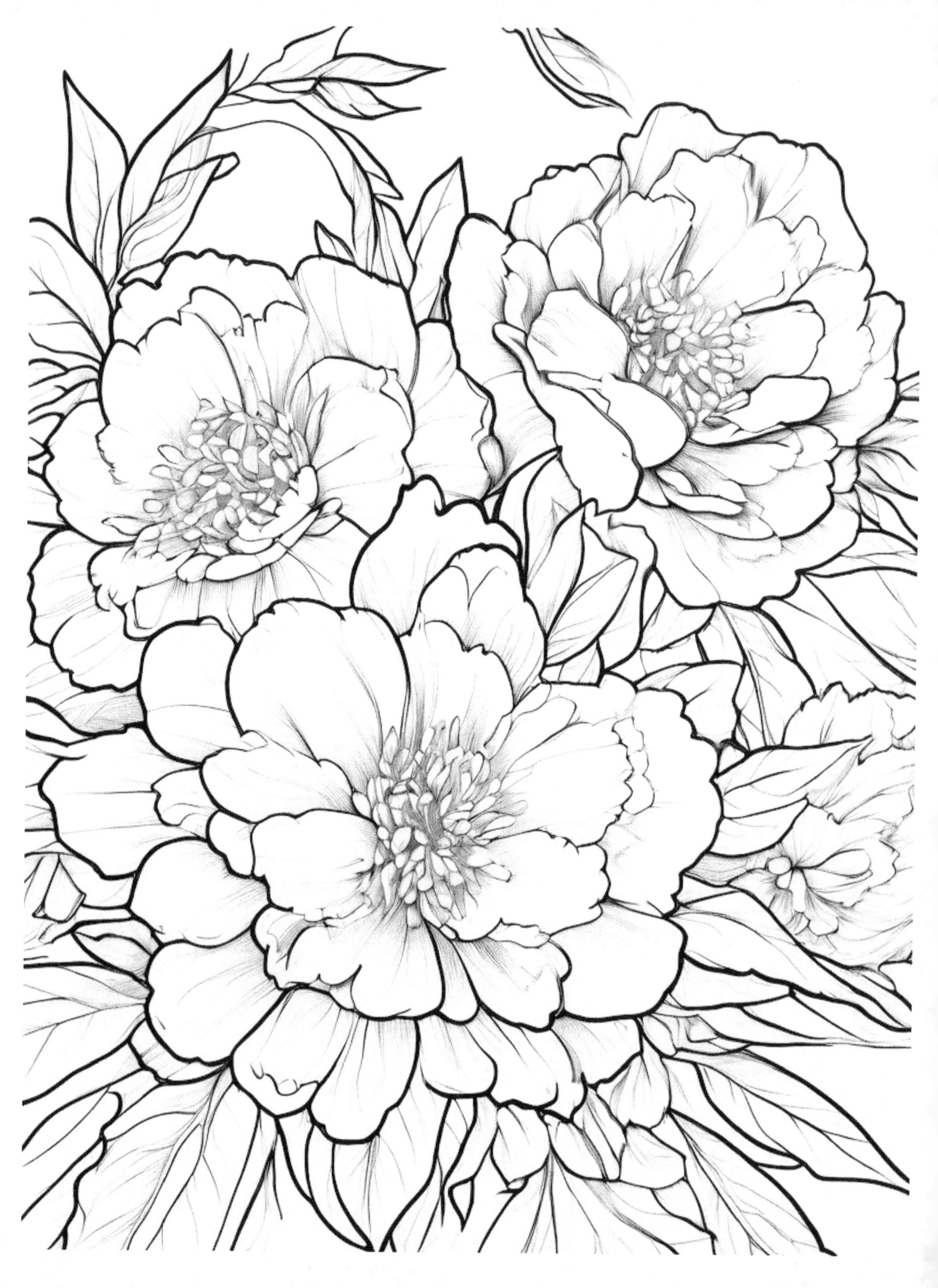

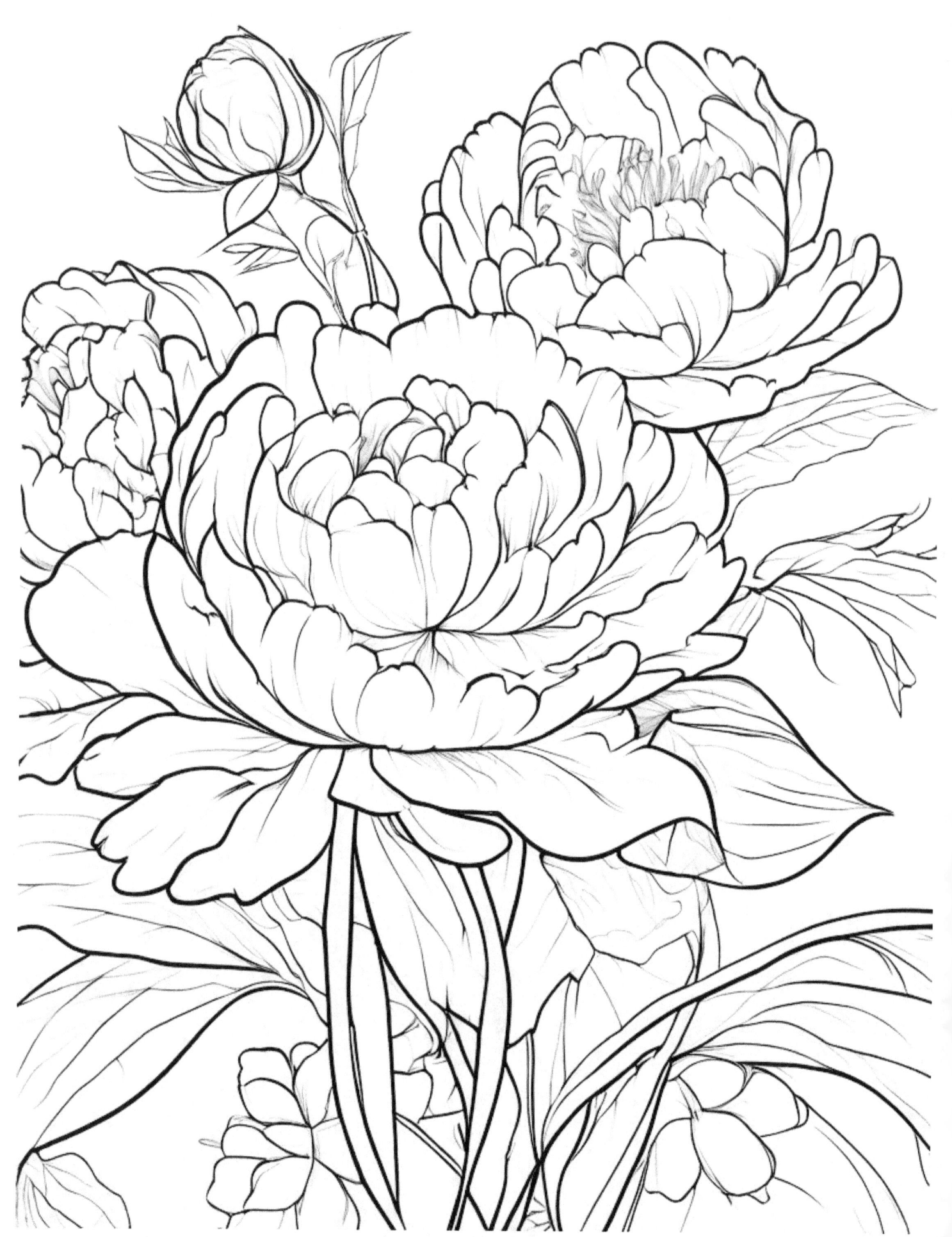

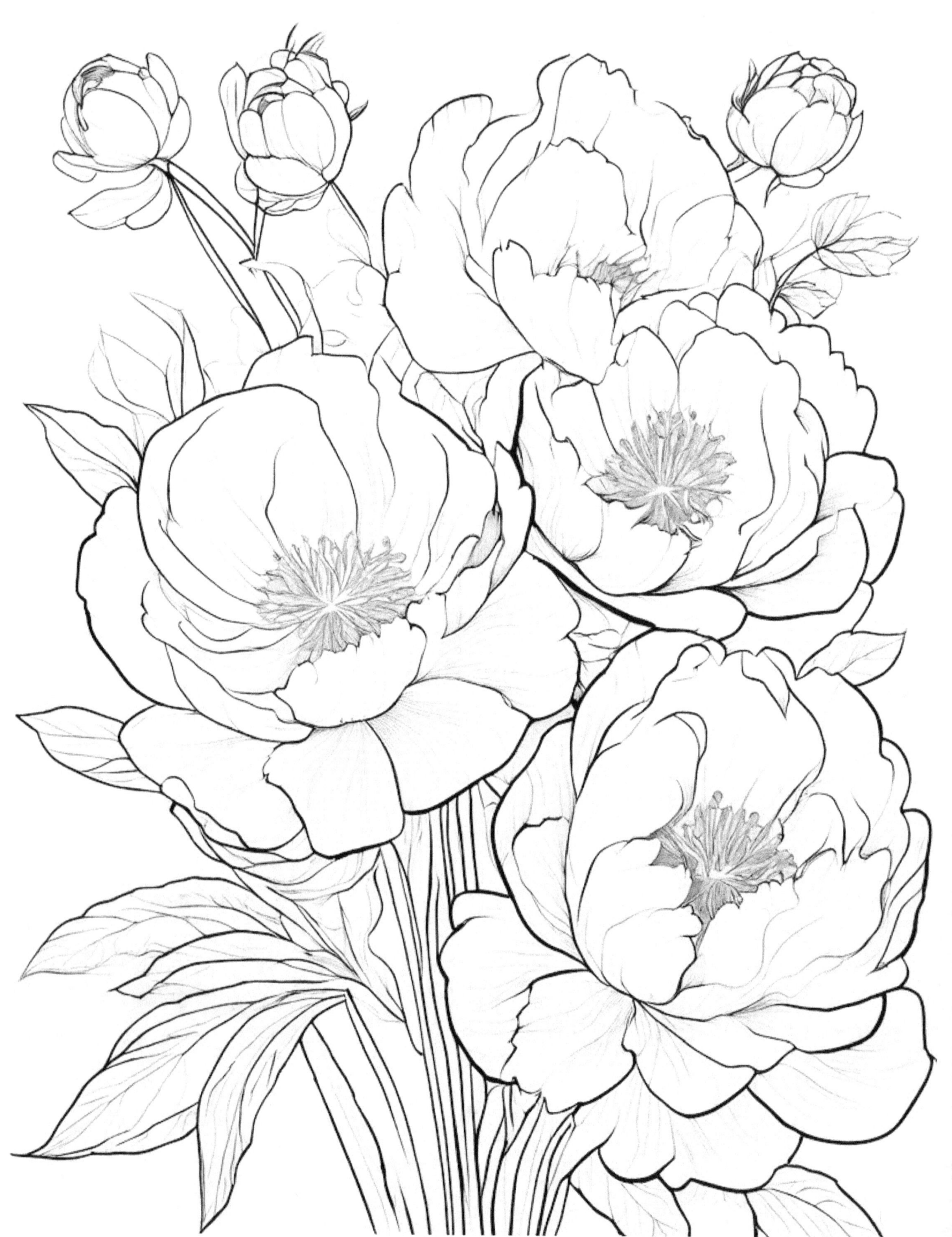

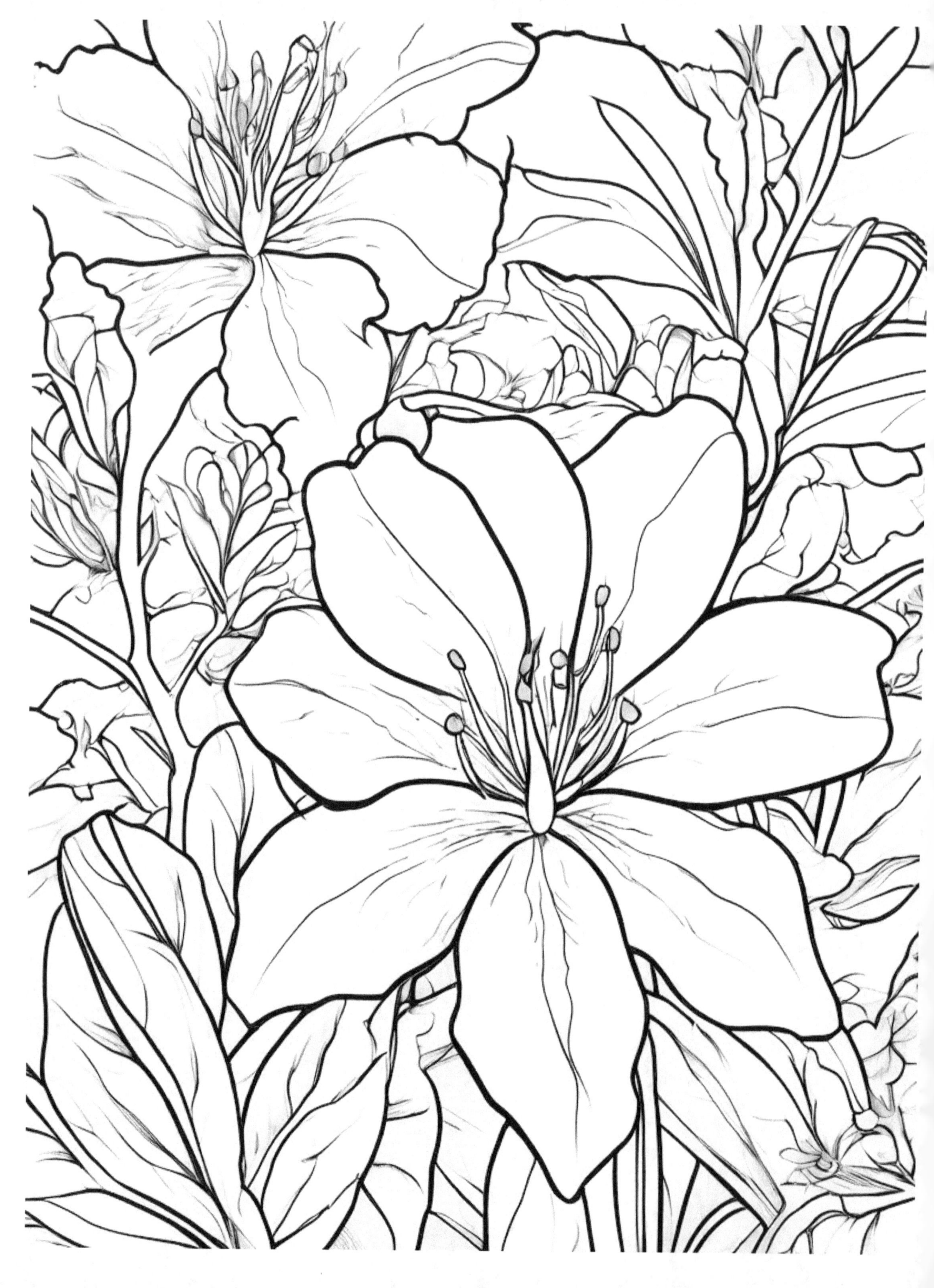

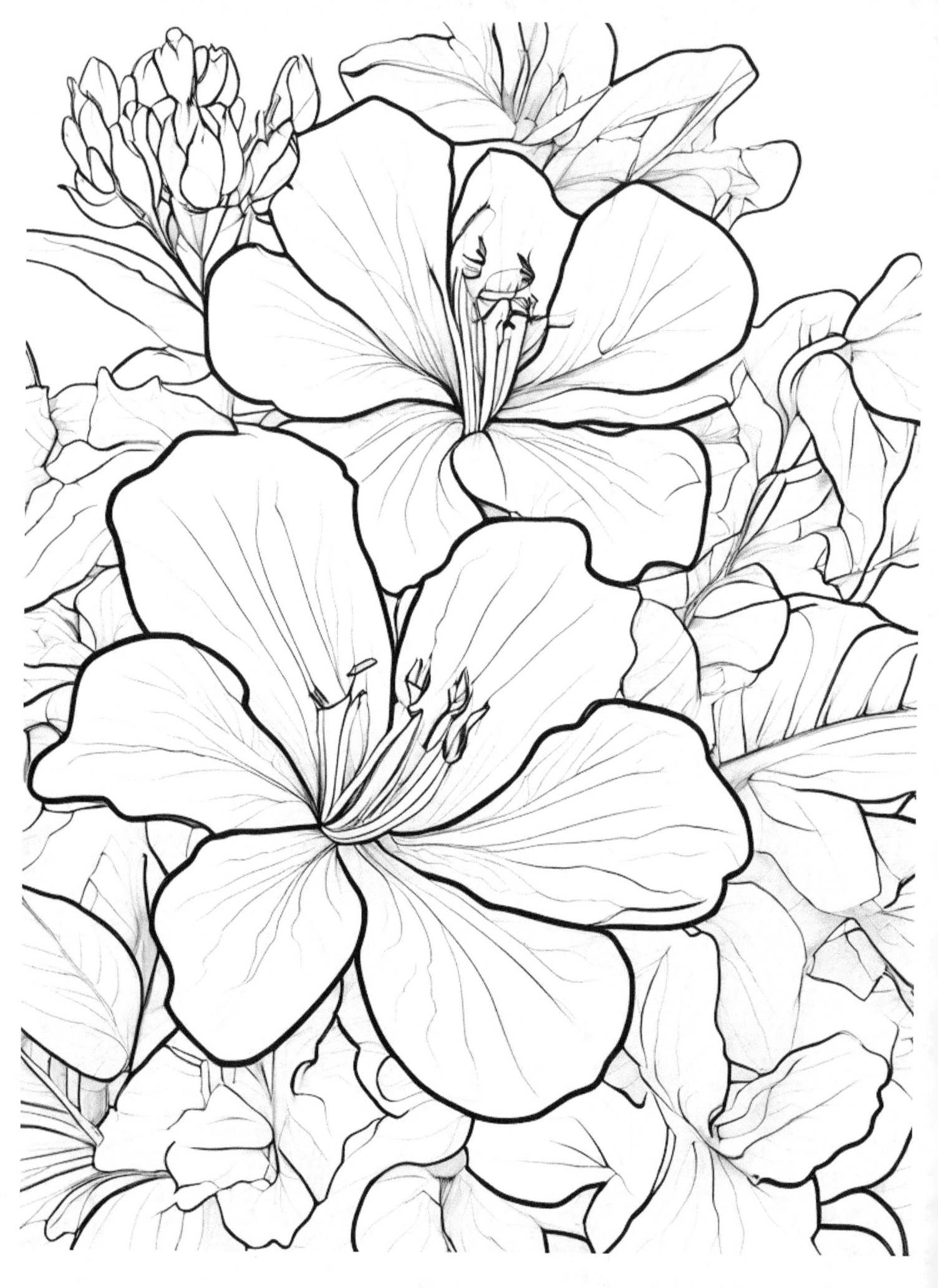

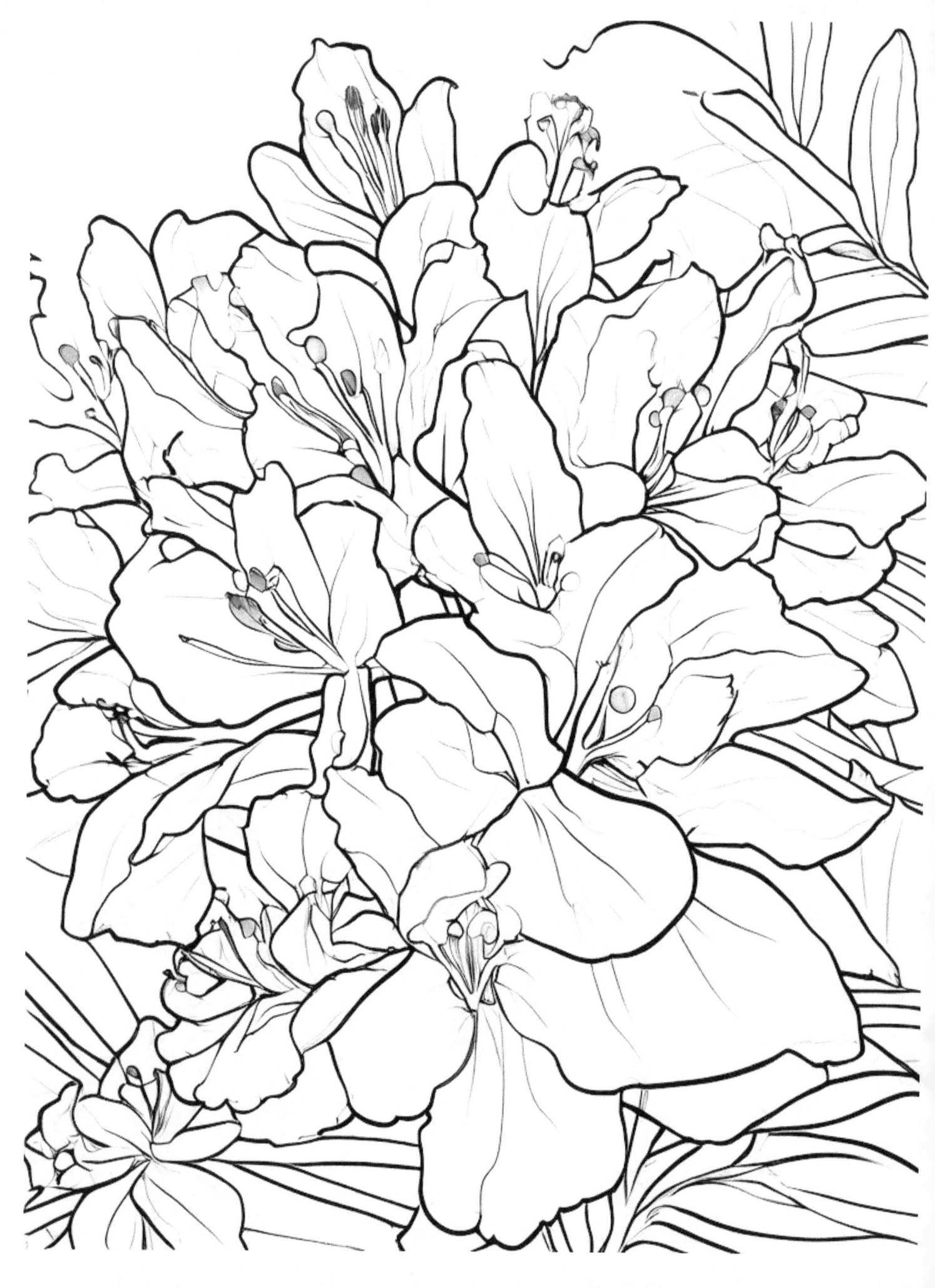

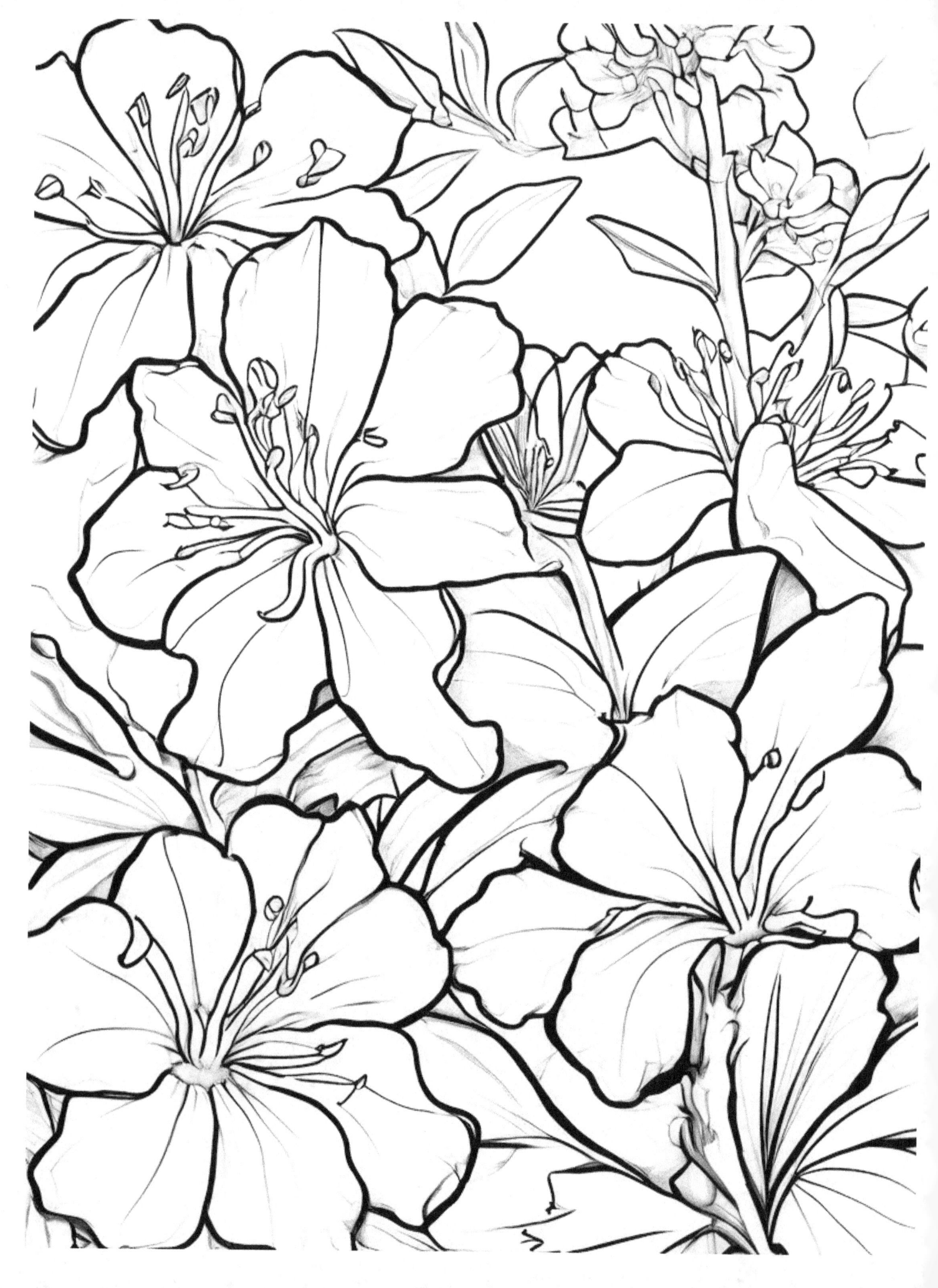

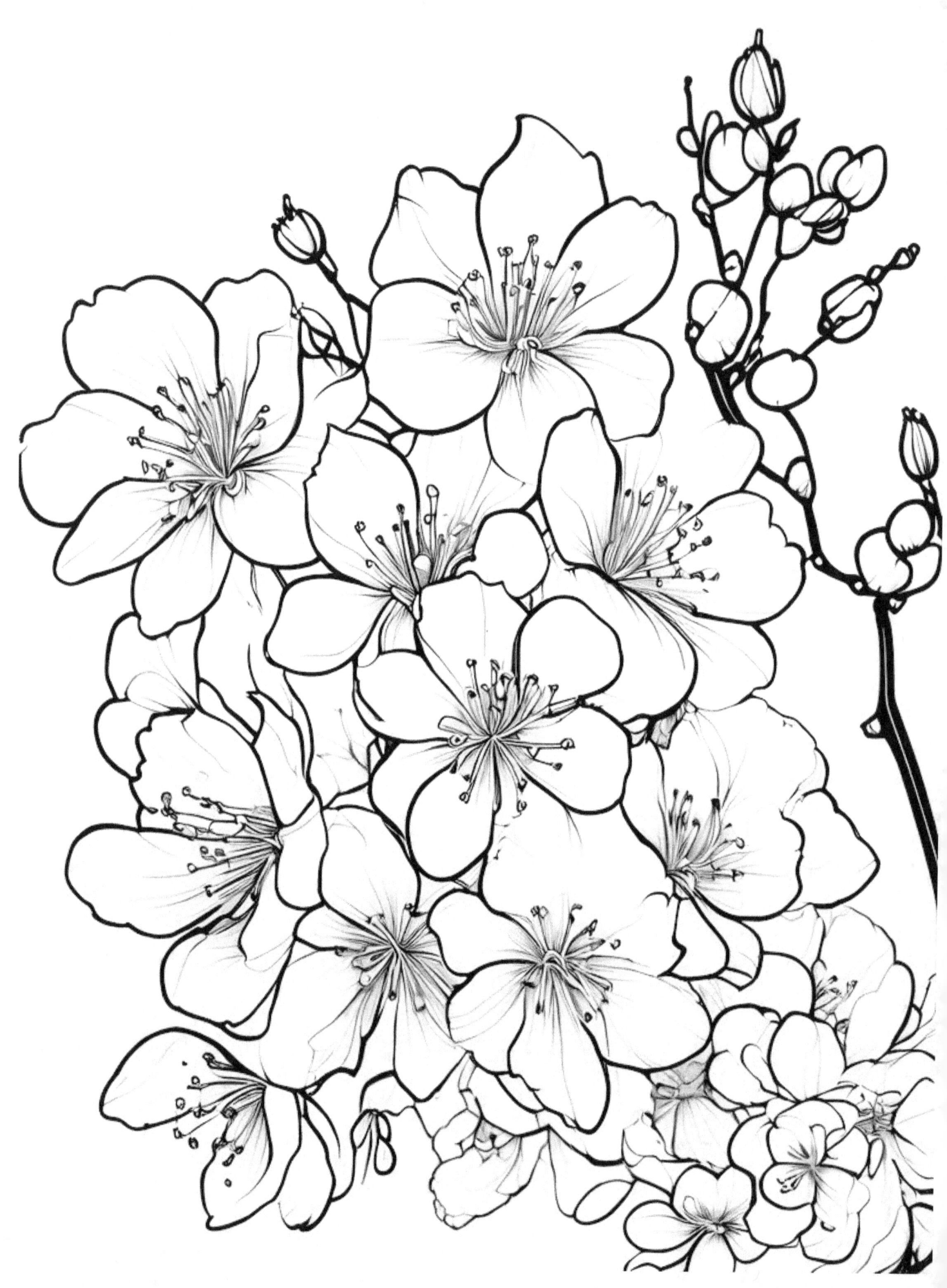

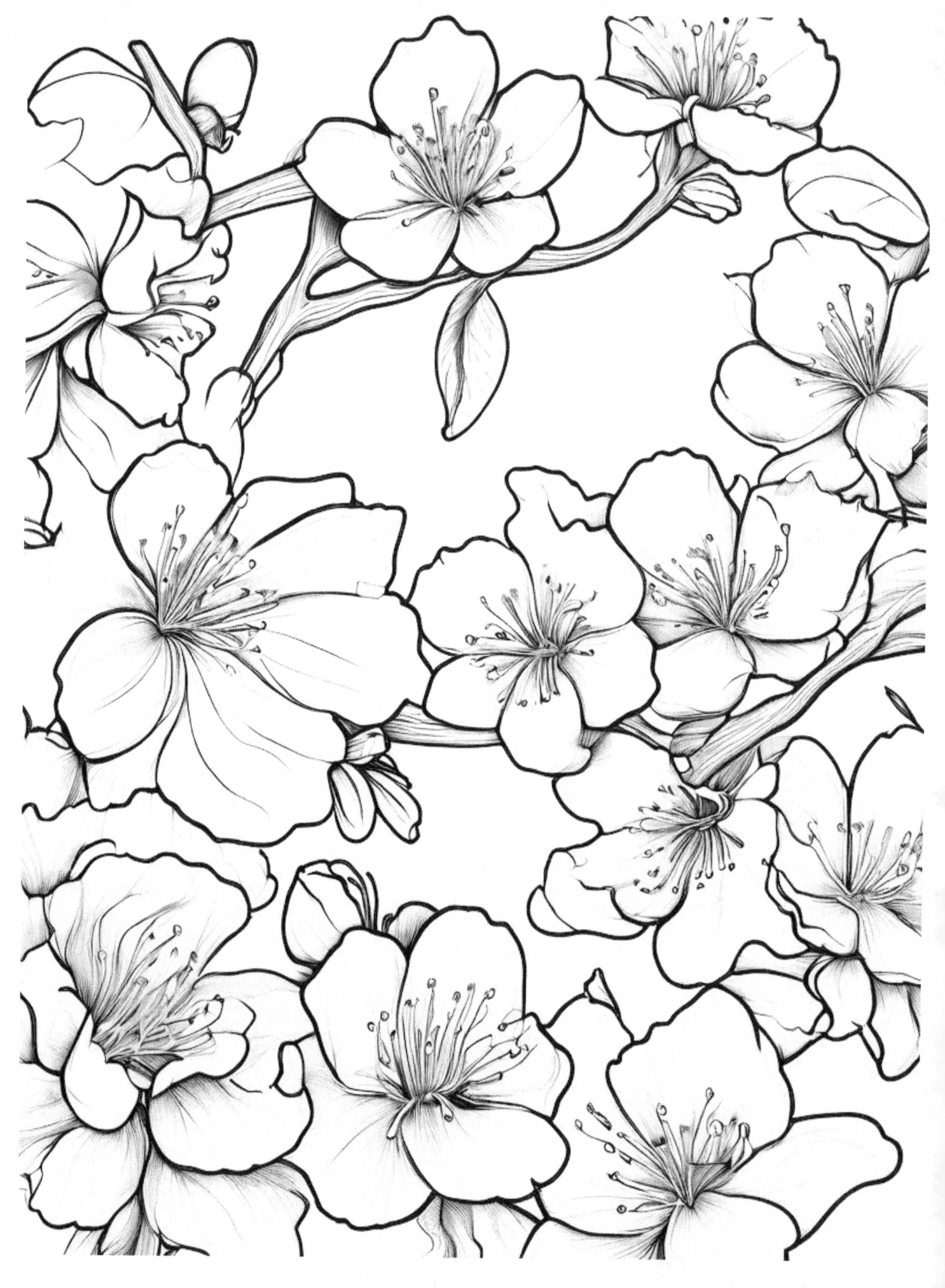

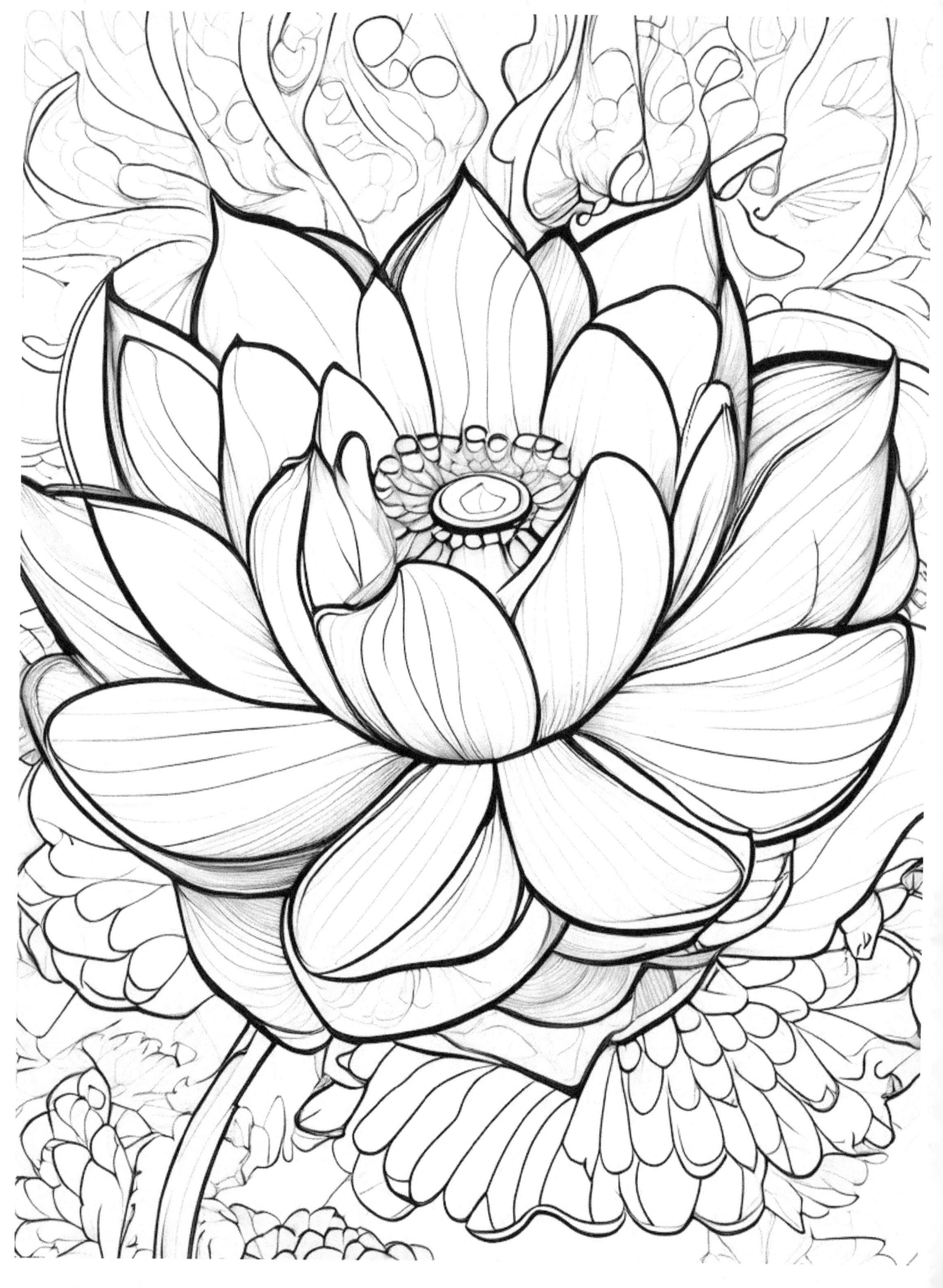

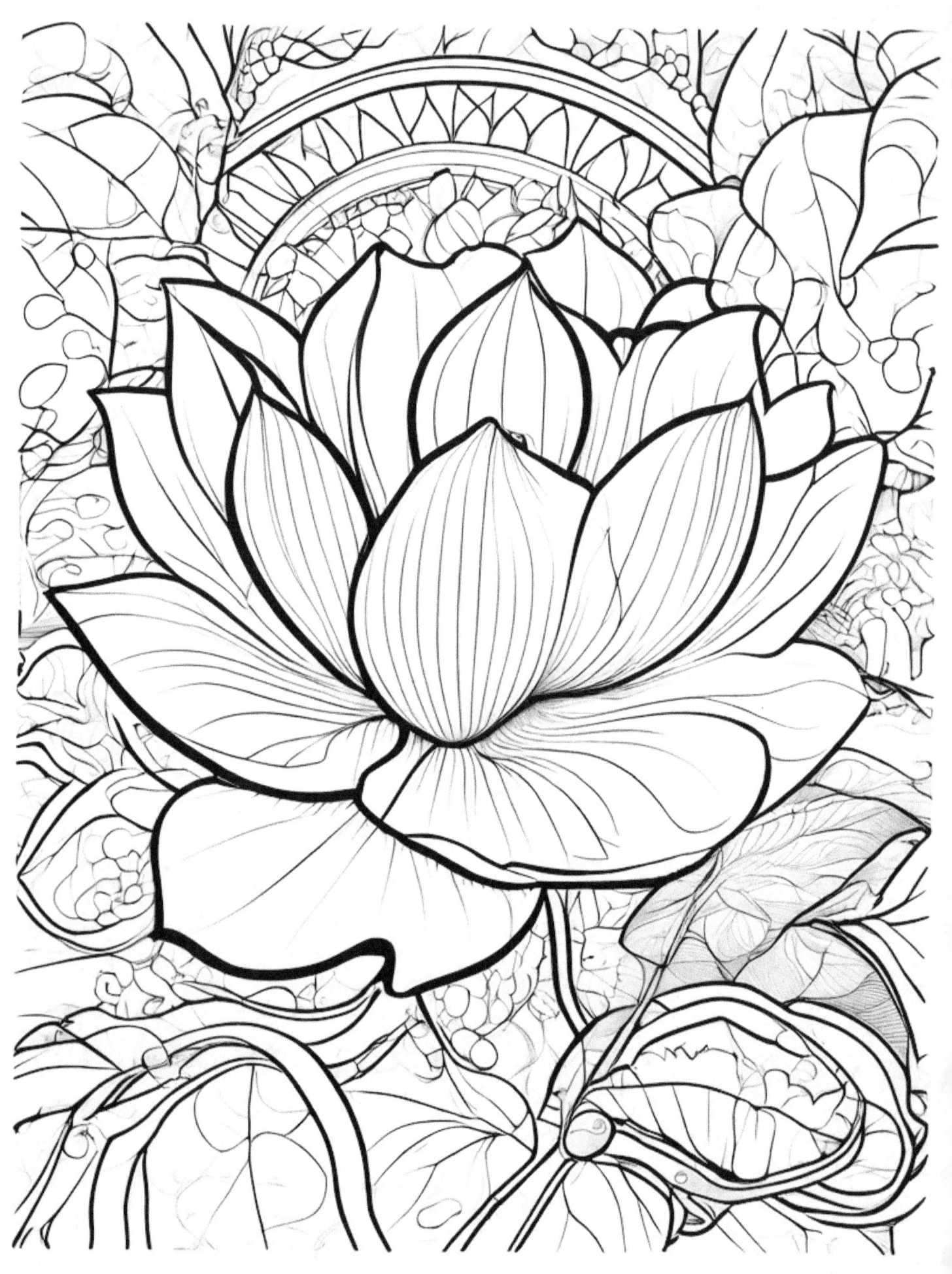

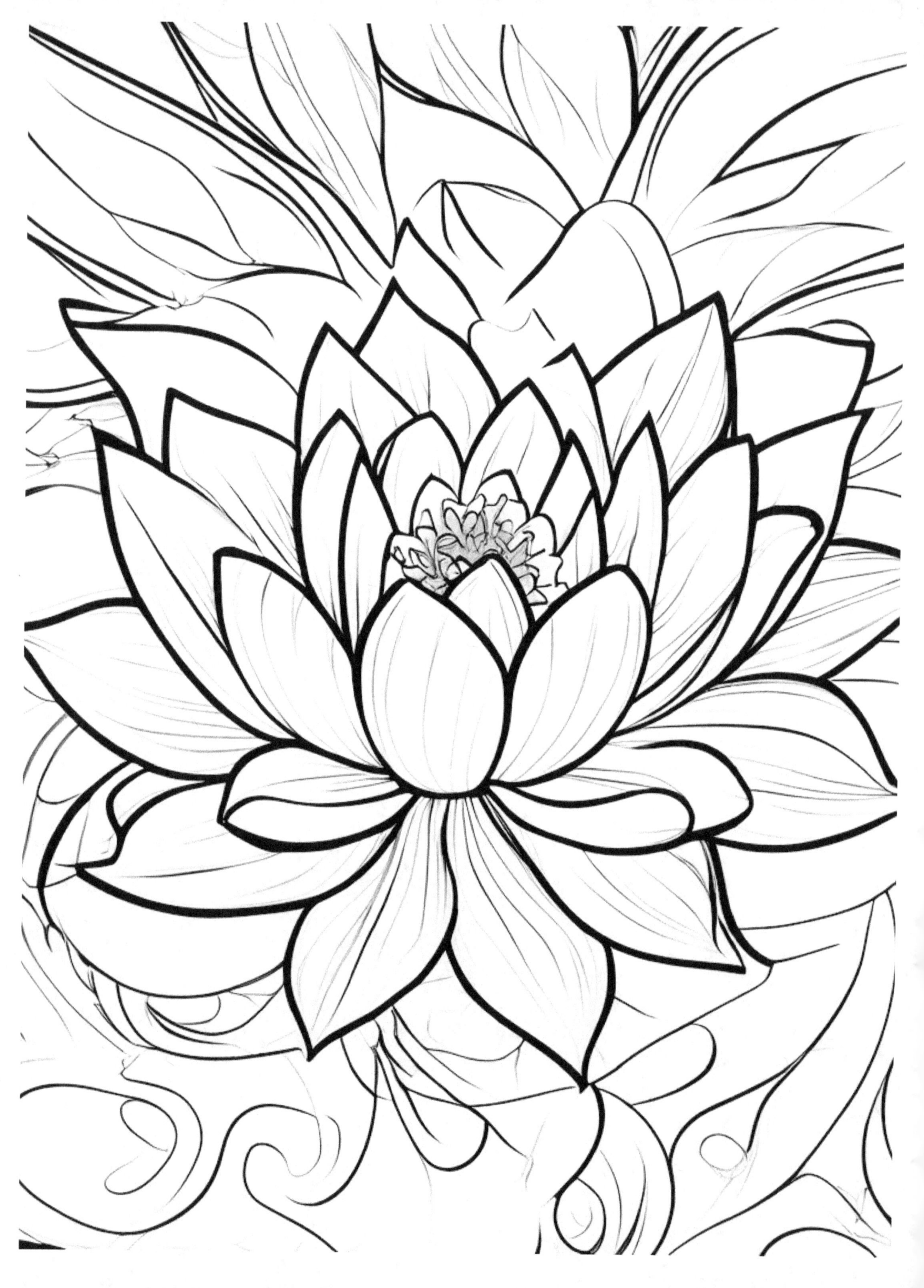

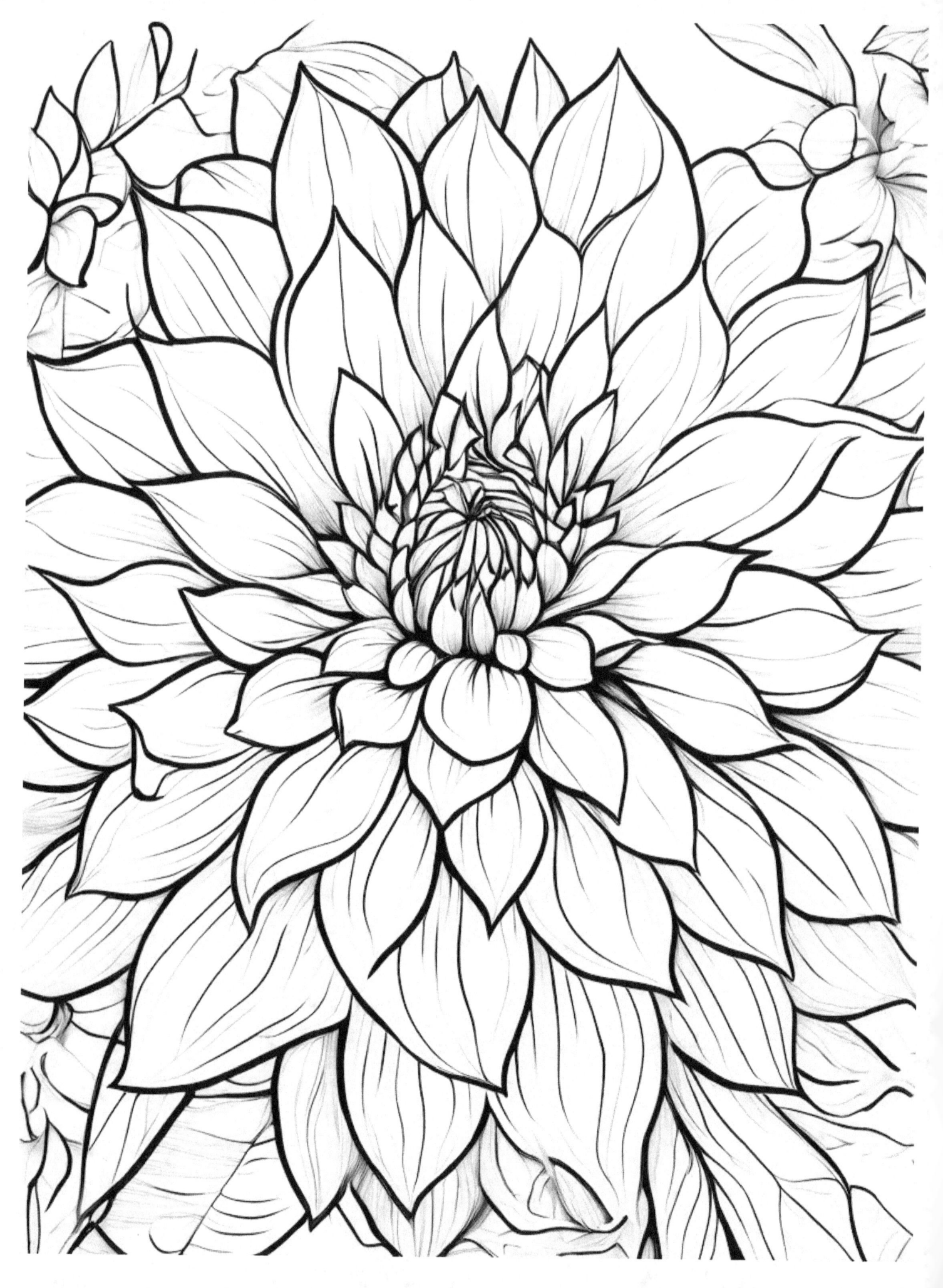

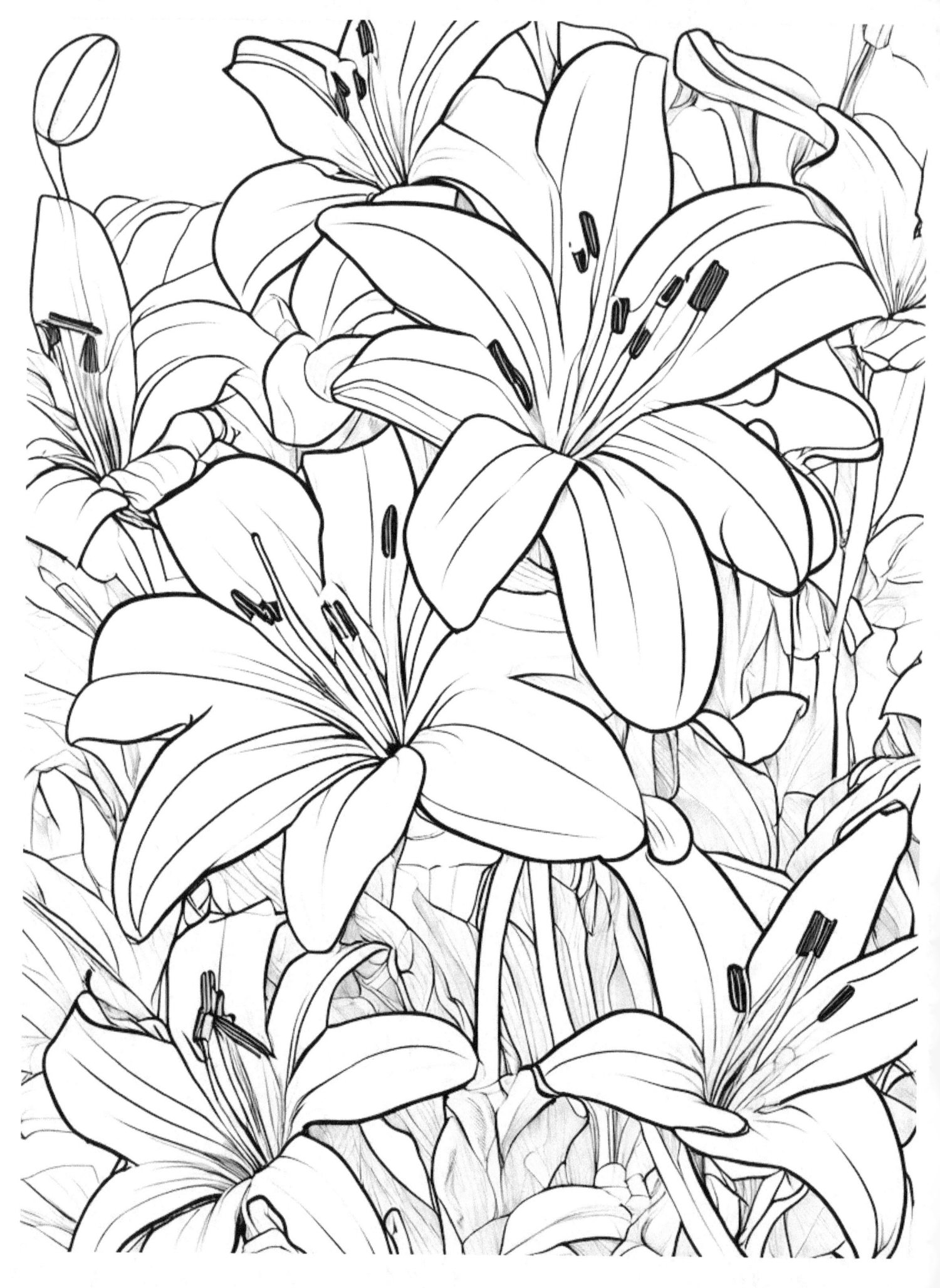

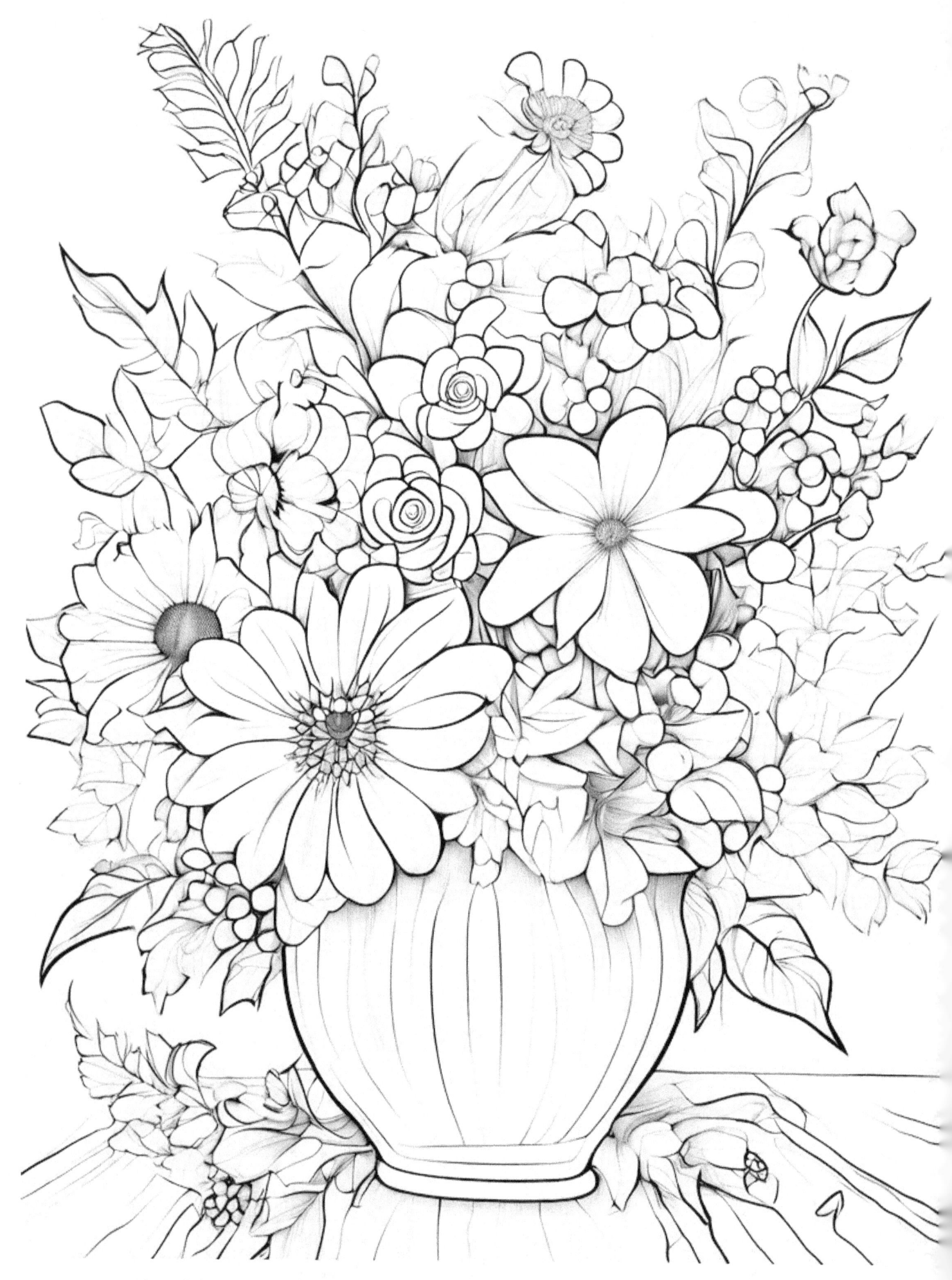

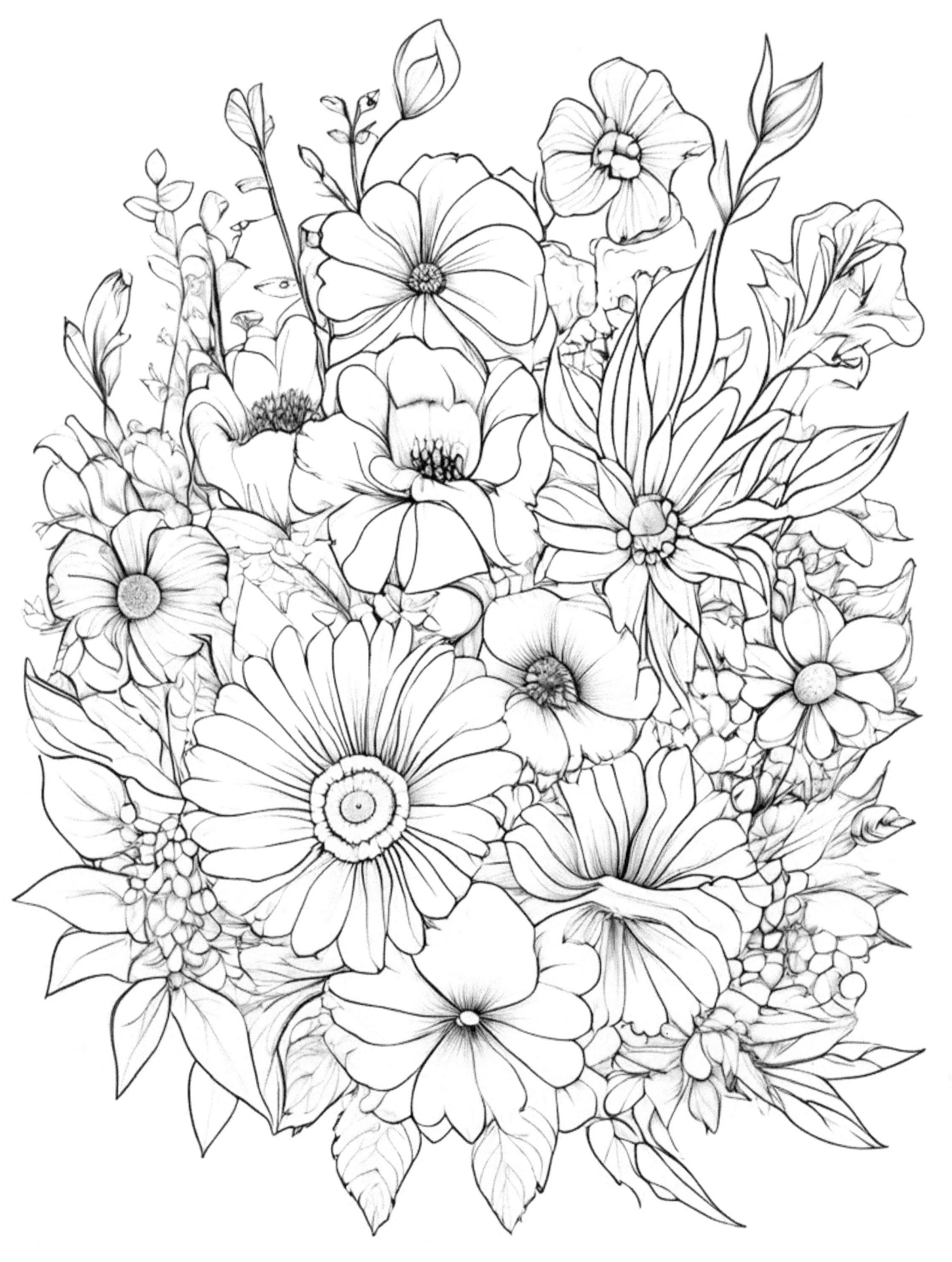

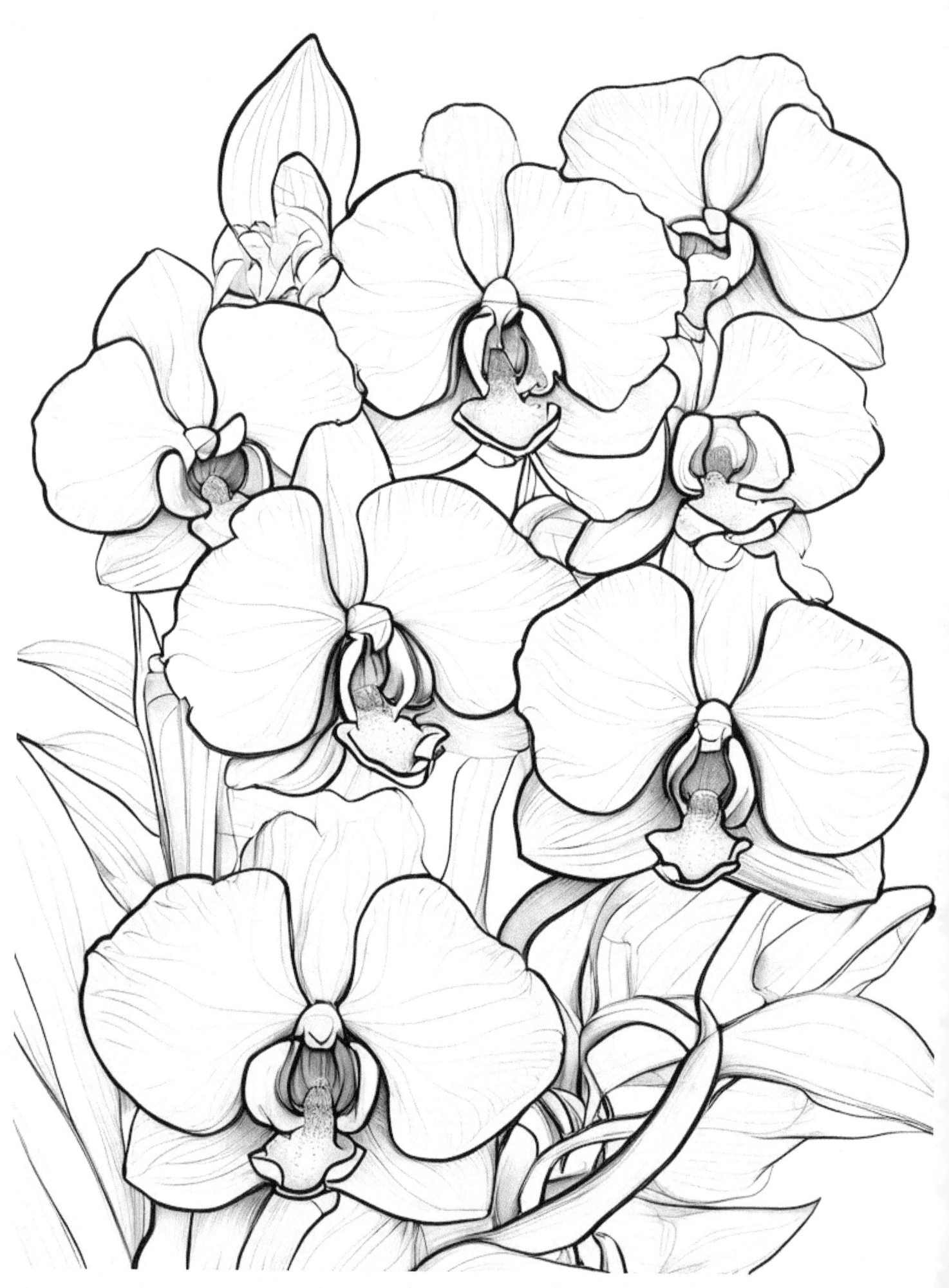

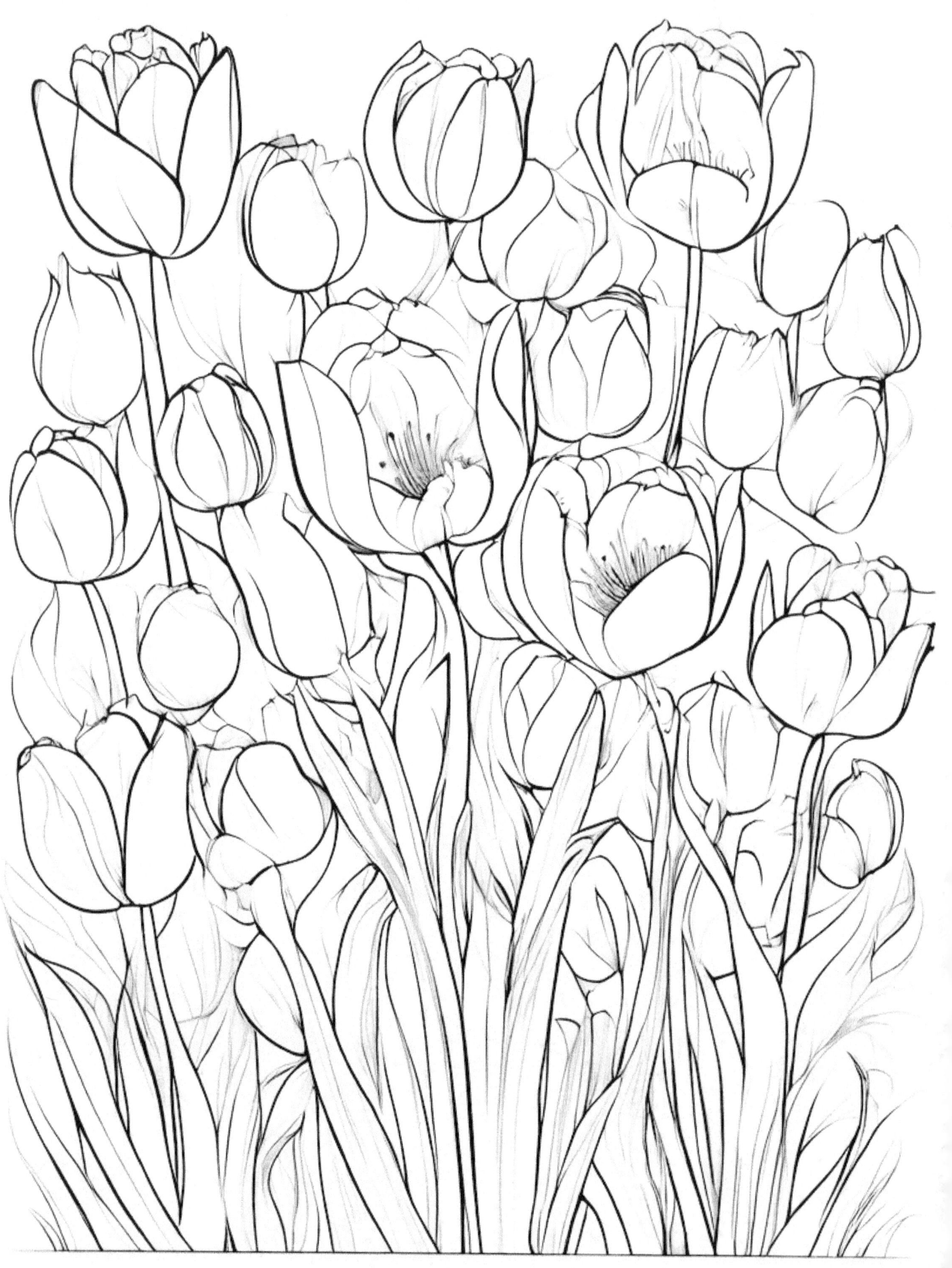

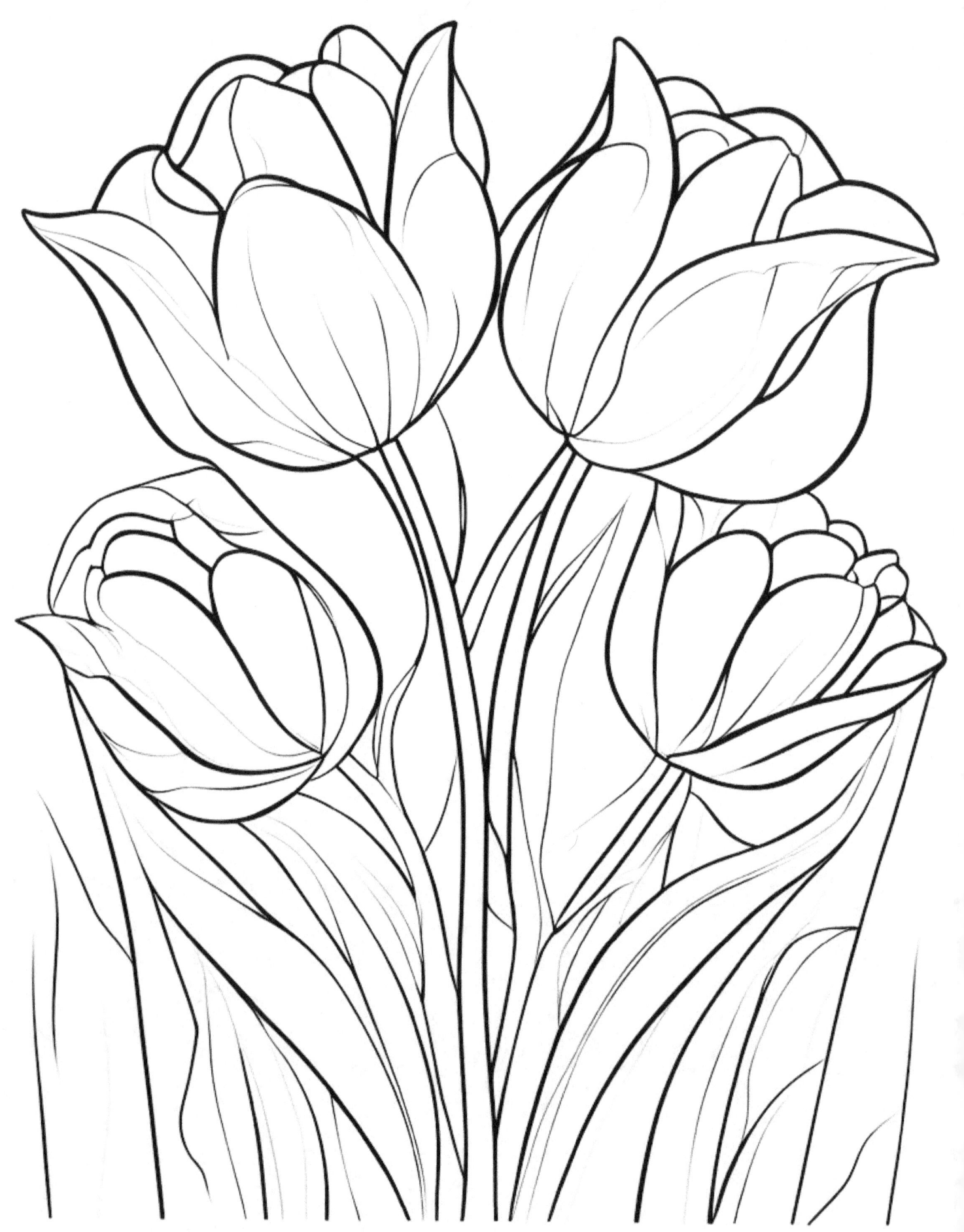

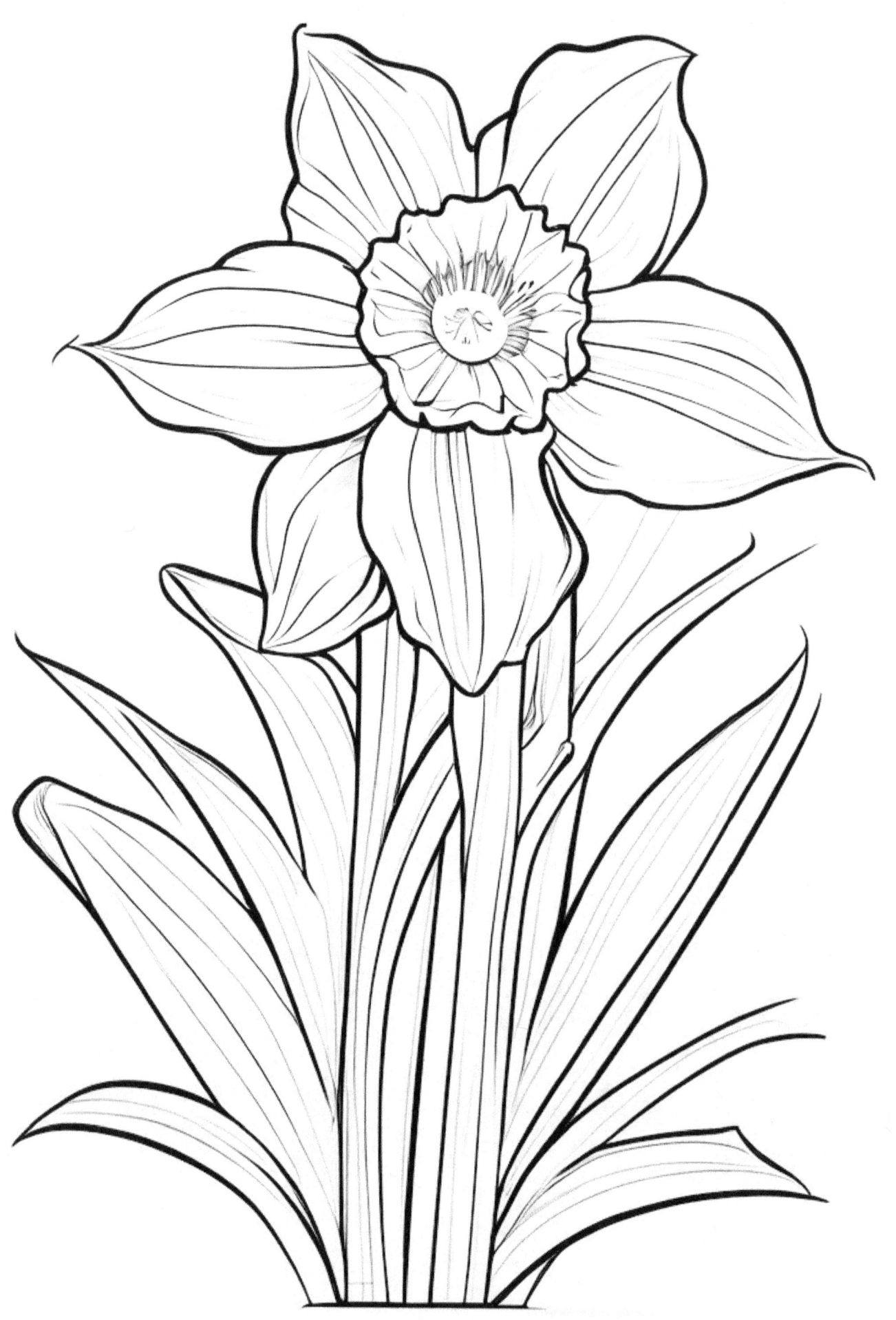